CFRE Exam Compass™
STUDY GUIDE

2023 Edition

EDITED BY Paula J. Jenkins, CFRE; Jeff Stanger; Eva Aldrich, Ph.D., CAE, (CFRE, 2001-2016)

PUBLISHED BY CFRE International

225 Reinekers Lane, Suite 625, Alexandria, VA 22314, USA

www.CFRE.org

© 2023 CFRE International

Cover by Cordy Gonzalez Art Direction & Design
Interior by Cordy Gonzalez Art Direction & Design
ISBN: 978-1-7347235-1-9

Made in the USA
Las Vegas, NV
05 November 2023

80290475R00044

It provides strategies for releasing fear through education, relaxation, and understanding the birthing process.

5. Ina May's Guide to Childbirth. (2018). Random House. (Original work published 2003)

Written by renowned midwife Ina May Gaskin, this popular book highlights the importance of creating a fear-free birthing environment. It offers personal stories, practical advice, and suggestions for releasing fear and promoting a positive childbirth experience.

Please visit my website at www.niaoaklandbetterbirthfoundation.com or find and like Oakland Better Birth Foundation on Facebook to receive notices of on our online classes and events that which will help you on your pregnancy / maternity journey.

My Youtube Channel, Better Birth TV, has even more information and inspiration for pregnant mommas and new parents!

2. Simkin, P., & Bolding, A. (2004). Update on Nonpharmacologic Approaches to Relieve Labour Pain and Prevent Suffering. Journal of Midwifery & Women's Health, 49(6), 489–504. https://doi.org/10.1016/j.jmwh.2004.09.010

This article discusses various nonpharmacological approaches to managing fear and pain during childbirth. It provides recommendations on techniques such as breathing exercises, relaxation techniques, and positive visualization.

3. Haines, H., Davis, D., & Neiman, E. (2015). Easing Labor Pain: The Neuroscience of Birth and the Role of Nonpharmacologic Approaches. The Journal of Perinatal Education, 24(4), 224–234. https://doi.org/10.1891/1058-1243.24.4.224

This article explores the neuroscience behind pain management during childbirth and emphasizes the importance of nonpharmacological approaches. It offers insights into releasing fear through evidence-based techniques.

4. Grantly Dick-Read. (2016). In Parenting for Peace. Penguin. (Original work published 1942)

This classic book by Grantly Dick-Read discusses the connection between fear and pain during childbirth.

READING LIST

Birth Without Fear by Grantly Dick Read
Ina May's Guide to Childbirth by Ina May Gaskin
The Birth Book
The Pregnancy Book by Sears and Sears

RESOURCES

Infant Mortality Rates in the USA
https://www.macrotrends.net/countries/USA/united-states/infant-mortality-rate

The Brewer Pregnancy Diet.
http://drbrewerpregnancydiet.com/index.html

Film: The Business of Being Born
www.thebusinessofbeingborn.com

1. Cook, R., Vedam, S., & Shazali, H. (2019). Releasing Fear in Childbirth: Understanding and Addressing Its Impact on Maternal and Infant Health. Journal of Perinatal Education, 28(1), 44–51. https://doi.org/10.1891/1058-1243.28.1.44

This scholarly article provides insights into the impact of fear on maternal and infant health during childbirth. It explores strategies to release fear and promote a positive birthing experience.

READING LIST

The Thinking Woman's Guide to a Better Birth - Henci Goer

Obstetric Myths Versus Research Realities - Henci Goer

Optimal Care in Childbirth - Henci Goer and Amy Romano

Childbirth Without Fear - Grantly Dick-Read

Heart and Hands &
Orgasmic Birth - Elizabeth Davis

Ina May's Guide to Childbirth.
Spiritual Midwifery, and
Ina May's Guide to Breastfeeding - Ina May Gaskin

The Doula Guide to Birth - Ananda Lowe & Rachel Zimmerman

Dr Jack Newman's Guide to Breastfeeding - Jack Newman MD

Baby's Are Not Pizzas - They are Born, Not Delivered - Rebecca Dekker Phd RN

The Birth Plan &
Birth. A Black Woman's Guide to Surviving and Thriving - visit www.niaoaklandbetterbirthfoundation.com for book release and purchase info.

NOTES FOR A
FEARLESS BIRTH

NOTES FOR A
FEARLESS BIRTH

NUTRITION

SUNDAY
Date:

Breakfast   Time:
Protein _____ Water __ Whole grain _____
Green Leafy Veg. _____
Vitamin C (from food) _____ additional
beverages and foods

_____

Lunch Time:
Protein _____ Water __ Whole grain _____
Green Leafy Veg. _____
Vitamin C (from food) _____ additional
beverages and foods

_____

Dinner   Time:
Protein _____ Water __ Whole grain _____
Green Leafy Veg. _____
Vitamin C (from food) _____ additional
beverages and foods

_____

How many 8oz glasses of water did I have today? Goal 10!

Notes or questions for my doula:

NUTRITION

SATURDAY

Date:

Breakfast   Time:

Protein _____ Water ___ Whole grain _____

Green Leafy Veg. _____

Vitamin C (from food) _____ additional
beverages and foods

_____

Lunch Time:

Protein _____ Water ___ Whole grain _____

Green Leafy Veg. _____

Vitamin C (from food) _____ additional
beverages and foods

_____

Dinner   Time:

Protein _____ Water ___ Whole grain _____

Green Leafy Veg. _____

Vitamin C (from food) _____ additional
beverages and foods

_____

How many 8oz glasses of water did I have today? Goal 10!

Notes or questions for my doula:

NUTRITION

FRIDAY
Date:

Breakfast   Time:
Protein _____ Water ___ Whole grain _____
Green Leafy Veg. _____
Vitamin C (from food) _____ additional
beverages and foods

_____

Lunch Time:
Protein _____ Water ___ Whole grain _____
Green Leafy Veg. _____
Vitamin C (from food) _____ additional
beverages and foods

_____

Dinner   Time:
Protein _____ Water ___ Whole grain _____
Green Leafy Veg. _____
Vitamin C (from food) _____ additional
beverages and foods

_____

How many 8oz glasses of water did I have today? Goal 10!

Notes or questions for my doula:

NUTRITION

THURSDAY

Date:

Breakfast   Time:

Protein _____ Water ___ Whole grain _____

Green Leafy Veg. _____

Vitamin C (from food) _____ additional
beverages and foods

_____

Lunch Time:

Protein _____ Water ___ Whole grain _____

Green Leafy Veg. _____

Vitamin C (from food) _____ additional
beverages and foods

_____

Dinner   Time:

Protein _____ Water ___ Whole grain _____

Green Leafy Veg. _____

Vitamin C (from food) _____ additional
beverages and foods

_____

How many 8oz glasses of water did I have today? Goal 10!

Notes or questions for my doula:

NUTRITION

WEDNESDAY

Date:

Breakfast   Time:

Protein _____ Water ___ Whole grain _____

Green Leafy Veg. _____

Vitamin C (from food) _____ additional
beverages and foods

_____

Lunch Time:

Protein _____ Water ___ Whole grain _____

Green Leafy Veg. _____

Vitamin C (from food) _____ additional
beverages and foods

_____

Dinner   Time:

Protein _____ Water ___ Whole grain _____

Green Leafy Veg. _____

Vitamin C (from food) _____ additional
beverages and foods

_____

How many 8oz glasses of water did I have today? Goal 10!

Notes or questions for my doula:

NUTRITION

TUESDAY
Date:

Breakfast   Time:

Protein _____ Water __ Whole grain _____
Green Leafy Veg. _____
Vitamin C (from food) _____ additional
beverages and foods

_____

Lunch Time:

Protein _____ Water __ Whole grain _____
Green Leafy Veg. _____
Vitamin C (from food) _____ additional
beverages and foods

_____

Dinner   Time:

Protein _____ Water __ Whole grain _____
Green Leafy Veg. _____
Vitamin C (from food) _____ additional
beverages and foods

_____

How many 8oz glasses of water did I have today? Goal 10!

Notes or questions for my doula:

NUTRITION

MONDAY

Date:

Breakfast   Time:

Protein _____ Water __ Whole grain _____

Green Leafy Veg. _____

Vitamin C (from food) _____ additional
beverages and foods

_____

Lunch Time:

Protein _____ Water __ Whole grain _____

Green Leafy Veg. _____

Vitamin C (from food) _____ additional
beverages and foods

_____

Dinner   Time:

Protein _____ Water __ Whole grain _____

Green Leafy Veg. _____

Vitamin C (from food) _____ additional
beverages and foods

_____

How many 8oz glasses of water did I have today? Goal 10!

Notes or questions for my doula:

NUTRITION

SUNDAY
Date:

Breakfast   Time:
Protein _____ Water __ Whole grain _____
Green Leafy Veg. _____
Vitamin C (from food) _____ additional
beverages and foods

_____

Lunch Time:
Protein _____ Water __ Whole grain _____
Green Leafy Veg. _____
Vitamin C (from food) _____ additional
beverages and foods

_____

Dinner   Time:
Protein _____ Water __ Whole grain _____
Green Leafy Veg. _____
Vitamin C (from food) _____ additional
beverages and foods

_____

How many 8oz glasses of water did I have today? Goal 10!

Notes or questions for my doula:

NUTRITION

SATURDAY
Date:

Breakfast   Time:
Protein _____ Water ___ Whole grain _____
Green Leafy Veg. _____
Vitamin C (from food) _____ additional
beverages and foods

_____

Lunch Time:
Protein _____ Water ___ Whole grain _____
Green Leafy Veg. _____
Vitamin C (from food) _____ additional
beverages and foods

_____

Dinner   Time:
Protein _____ Water ___ Whole grain _____
Green Leafy Veg. _____
Vitamin C (from food) _____ additional
beverages and foods

_____

How many 8oz glasses of water did I have today? Goal 10!

Notes or questions for my doula:

NUTRITION

FRIDAY

Date:

Breakfast   Time:

Protein _____ Water ___ Whole grain _____

Green Leafy Veg. _____

Vitamin C (from food) _____ additional
beverages and foods

_____

Lunch Time:

Protein _____ Water ___ Whole grain _____

Green Leafy Veg. _____

Vitamin C (from food) _____ additional
beverages and foods

_____

Dinner   Time:

Protein _____ Water ___ Whole grain _____

Green Leafy Veg. _____

Vitamin C (from food) _____ additional
beverages and foods

_____

How many 8oz glasses of water did I have today? Goal 10!

Notes or questions for my doula:

NUTRITION

THURSDAY
Date:

Breakfast   Time:
Protein _____ Water __ Whole grain _____
Green Leafy Veg. _____
Vitamin C (from food) _____ additional
beverages and foods

_____

Lunch Time:
Protein _____ Water __ Whole grain _____
Green Leafy Veg. _____
Vitamin C (from food) _____ additional
beverages and foods

_____

Dinner   Time:
Protein _____ Water __ Whole grain _____
Green Leafy Veg. _____
Vitamin C (from food) _____ additional
beverages and foods

_____

How many 8oz glasses of water did I have today? Goal 10!

Notes or questions for my doula:

NUTRITION

WEDNESDAY

Date:

Breakfast   Time:

Protein _____ Water ___ Whole grain _____

Green Leafy Veg. _____

Vitamin C (from food) _____ additional
beverages and foods

_____

Lunch Time:

Protein _____ Water ___ Whole grain _____

Green Leafy Veg. _____

Vitamin C (from food) _____ additional
beverages and foods

_____

Dinner   Time:

Protein _____ Water ___ Whole grain _____

Green Leafy Veg. _____

Vitamin C (from food) _____ additional
beverages and foods

_____

How many 8oz glasses of water did I have today? Goal 10!

Notes or questions for my doula:

NUTRITION

TUESDAY
Date:

Breakfast   Time:
Protein _____ Water __ Whole grain _____
Green Leafy Veg. _____
Vitamin C (from food) _____ additional
beverages and foods

_____

Lunch Time:
Protein _____ Water __ Whole grain _____
Green Leafy Veg. _____
Vitamin C (from food) _____ additional
beverages and foods

_____

Dinner   Time:
Protein _____ Water __ Whole grain _____
Green Leafy Veg. _____
Vitamin C (from food) _____ additional
beverages and foods

_____

How many 8oz glasses of water did I have today? Goal 10!

Notes or questions for my doula:

NUTRITION

MONDAY

Date:

Breakfast   Time:

Protein _____ Water ___ Whole grain _____

Green Leafy Veg. _____

Vitamin C (from food) _____ additional

beverages and foods

_____

Lunch Time:

Protein _____ Water ___ Whole grain _____

Green Leafy Veg. _____

Vitamin C (from food) _____ additional

beverages and foods

_____

Dinner   Time:

Protein _____ Water ___ Whole grain _____

Green Leafy Veg. _____

Vitamin C (from food) _____ additional

beverages and foods

_____

How many 8oz glasses of water did I have today? Goal 10!

Notes or questions for my doula:

NUTRITION

SUNDAY
Date:

Breakfast   Time:
Protein _____ Water ___ Whole grain _____
Green Leafy Veg. _____
Vitamin C (from food) _____ additional
beverages and foods

_____

Lunch Time:
Protein _____ Water ___ Whole grain _____
Green Leafy Veg. _____
Vitamin C (from food) _____ additional
beverages and foods

_____

Dinner   Time:
Protein _____ Water ___ Whole grain _____
Green Leafy Veg. _____
Vitamin C (from food) _____ additional
beverages and foods

_____

How many 8oz glasses of water did I have today? Goal 10!

Notes or questions for my doula:

NUTRITION

SATURDAY

Date:

Breakfast   Time:

Protein _____ Water __ Whole grain _____

Green Leafy Veg. _____

Vitamin C (from food) _____ additional
beverages and foods

_____

Lunch Time:

Protein _____ Water __ Whole grain _____

Green Leafy Veg. _____

Vitamin C (from food) _____ additional
beverages and foods

_____

Dinner   Time:

Protein _____ Water __ Whole grain _____

Green Leafy Veg. _____

Vitamin C (from food) _____ additional
beverages and foods

_____

How many 8oz glasses of water did I have today? Goal 10!

Notes or questions for my doula:

NUTRITION

FRIDAY

Date:

Breakfast   Time:

Protein _____ Water ___ Whole grain _____

Green Leafy Veg. _____

Vitamin C (from food) _____ additional

beverages and foods

_____

Lunch Time:

Protein _____ Water ___ Whole grain _____

Green Leafy Veg. _____

Vitamin C (from food) _____ additional

beverages and foods

_____

Dinner   Time:

Protein _____ Water ___ Whole grain _____

Green Leafy Veg. _____

Vitamin C (from food) _____ additional

beverages and foods

_____

How many 8oz glasses of water did I have today? Goal 10!

Notes or questions for my doula:

NUTRITION

THURSDAY

Date:

Breakfast   Time:

Protein _____ Water ___ Whole grain _____

Green Leafy Veg. _____

Vitamin C (from food) _____ additional
beverages and foods

_____

Lunch Time:

Protein _____ Water ___ Whole grain _____

Green Leafy Veg. _____

Vitamin C (from food) _____ additional
beverages and foods

_____

Dinner   Time:

Protein _____ Water ___ Whole grain _____

Green Leafy Veg. _____

Vitamin C (from food) _____ additional
beverages and foods

_____

How many 8oz glasses of water did I have today? Goal 10!

Notes or questions for my doula:

NUTRITION

WEDNESDAY
Date:

Breakfast   Time:
Protein _____ Water ___ Whole grain _____
Green Leafy Veg. _____
Vitamin C (from food) _____ additional
beverages and foods

_____

Lunch Time:
Protein _____ Water ___ Whole grain _____
Green Leafy Veg. _____
Vitamin C (from food) _____ additional
beverages and foods

_____

Dinner   Time:
Protein _____ Water ___ Whole grain _____
Green Leafy Veg. _____
Vitamin C (from food) _____ additional
beverages and foods

_____

How many 8oz glasses of water did I have today? Goal 10!

Notes or questions for my doula:

NUTRITION

TUESDAY
Date:

Breakfast   Time:
Protein _____ Water ___ Whole grain _____
Green Leafy Veg. _____
Vitamin C (from food) _____ additional
beverages and foods

_____

Lunch Time:
Protein _____ Water ___ Whole grain _____
Green Leafy Veg. _____
Vitamin C (from food) _____ additional
beverages and foods

_____

Dinner   Time:
Protein _____ Water ___ Whole grain _____
Green Leafy Veg. _____
Vitamin C (from food) _____ additional
beverages and foods

_____

How many 8oz glasses of water did I have today? Goal 10!

Notes or questions for my doula:

NUTRITION

MONDAY
Date:

Breakfast   Time:
Protein _____ Water __ Whole grain _____
Green Leafy Veg. _____
Vitamin C (from food) _____ additional
beverages and foods

_____

Lunch Time:
Protein _____ Water __ Whole grain _____
Green Leafy Veg. _____
Vitamin C (from food) _____ additional
beverages and foods

_____

Dinner   Time:
Protein _____ Water __ Whole grain _____
Green Leafy Veg. _____
Vitamin C (from food) _____ additional
beverages and foods

_____

How many 8oz glasses of water did I have today? Goal 10!

Notes or questions for my doula:

NUTRITION

SUNDAY

Date:

Breakfast   Time:

Protein _____ Water ___ Whole grain _____

Green Leafy Veg. _____

Vitamin C (from food) _____ additional
beverages and foods

_____

Lunch Time:

Protein _____ Water ___ Whole grain _____

Green Leafy Veg. _____

Vitamin C (from food) _____ additional
beverages and foods

_____

Dinner   Time:

Protein _____ Water ___ Whole grain _____

Green Leafy Veg. _____

Vitamin C (from food) _____ additional
beverages and foods

_____

How many 8oz glasses of water did I have today? Goal 10!

Notes or questions for my doula:

NUTRITION

SATURDAY
Date:

Breakfast   Time:
Protein _____ Water ___ Whole grain _____
Green Leafy Veg. _____
Vitamin C (from food) _____ additional
beverages and foods

_____

Lunch Time:
Protein _____ Water ___ Whole grain _____
Green Leafy Veg. _____
Vitamin C (from food) _____ additional
beverages and foods

_____

Dinner   Time:
Protein _____ Water ___ Whole grain _____
Green Leafy Veg. _____
Vitamin C (from food) _____ additional
beverages and foods

_____

How many 8oz glasses of water did I have today? Goal 10!

Notes or questions for my doula:

NUTRITION

FRIDAY

Date:

Breakfast   Time:

Protein _____ Water __ Whole grain _____

Green Leafy Veg. _____

Vitamin C (from food) _____ additional
beverages and foods

_____

Lunch Time:

Protein _____ Water __ Whole grain _____

Green Leafy Veg. _____

Vitamin C (from food) _____ additional
beverages and foods

_____

Dinner   Time:

Protein _____ Water __ Whole grain _____

Green Leafy Veg. _____

Vitamin C (from food) _____ additional
beverages and foods

_____

How many 8oz glasses of water did I have today? Goal 10!

Notes or questions for my doula:

NUTRITION

THURSDAY
Date:

Breakfast   Time:
Protein _____ Water ___ Whole grain _____
Green Leafy Veg. _____
Vitamin C (from food) _____ additional
beverages and foods

_____

Lunch Time:
Protein _____ Water ___ Whole grain _____
Green Leafy Veg. _____
Vitamin C (from food) _____ additional
beverages and foods

_____

Dinner   Time:
Protein _____ Water ___ Whole grain _____
Green Leafy Veg. _____
Vitamin C (from food) _____ additional
beverages and foods

_____

How many 8oz glasses of water did I have today? Goal 10!

Notes or questions for my doula:

NUTRITION

WEDNESDAY

Date:

Breakfast   Time:

Protein _____ Water ___ Whole grain _____

Green Leafy Veg. _____

Vitamin C (from food) _____ additional

beverages and foods

_____

Lunch Time:

Protein _____ Water ___ Whole grain _____

Green Leafy Veg. _____

Vitamin C (from food) _____ additional

beverages and foods

_____

Dinner   Time:

Protein _____ Water ___ Whole grain _____

Green Leafy Veg. _____

Vitamin C (from food) _____ additional

beverages and foods

_____

How many 8oz glasses of water did I have today? Goal 10!

Notes or questions for my doula:

NUTRITION

TUESDAY
Date:

Breakfast   Time:
Protein _____ Water ___ Whole grain _____
Green Leafy Veg. _____
Vitamin C (from food) _____ additional
beverages and foods

_____

Lunch Time:
Protein _____ Water ___ Whole grain _____
Green Leafy Veg. _____
Vitamin C (from food) _____ additional
beverages and foods

_____

Dinner   Time:
Protein _____ Water ___ Whole grain _____
Green Leafy Veg. _____
Vitamin C (from food) _____ additional
beverages and foods

_____

How many 8oz glasses of water did I have today? Goal 10!

Notes or questions for my doula:

NUTRITION

MONDAY

Date:

Breakfast   Time:

Protein _____ Water ___ Whole grain _____

Green Leafy Veg. _____

Vitamin C (from food) _____ additional
beverages and foods

_____

Lunch Time:

Protein _____ Water ___ Whole grain _____

Green Leafy Veg. _____

Vitamin C (from food) _____ additional
beverages and foods

_____

Dinner   Time:

Protein _____ Water ___ Whole grain _____

Green Leafy Veg. _____

Vitamin C (from food) _____ additional
beverages and foods

_____

How many 8oz glasses of water did I have today? Goal 10!

Notes or questions for my doula:

YOUR BIRTH TEAM

NOTES

YOUR BIRTH TEAM
NOTES

YOUR BIRTH STORY

_____

_____

_____

_____

_____

_____

_____

_____

_____

_____

_____

_____

_____

_____

_____

_____

_____

_____

_____

_____

_____

_____

_____

_____

YOUR BIRTH STORY

YOUR BIRTH STORY

YOUR BIRTH STORY

_____
_____
_____
_____
_____
_____
_____
_____
_____
_____
_____
_____
_____
_____
_____
_____
_____
_____
_____
_____
_____
_____
_____

YOUR BIRTH STORY

YOUR BIRTH STORY

No one can tell you how your labor will go - we can only share with you the probable experience of a healthy laboring woman. What we know is that the average length of labor for a first-time mother is about 24 hours.

24 hours. 1 day. You can do this. Even if it's longer, your amazing body and your amazing baby - can do this!
Any questions? Please don't hesitate to reach out to me. Oaklandbetterbirthfoundation@gmail.com

I'm holding you and your family in love and light.

Peace, and Baby Blessings to you!

There is a bit of faith required in the process. Faith that you can do what's needed to keep your healthy body healthy throughout your pregnancy. Faith that you can choose providers who support your desires and birth vision and who can walk with you to your destination of motherhood/parenthood.

Courage is required, in pregnancy as well as in parenting. Your birth team ought to encourage your courageousness rather than feed your fears.

And with all this support in place, it will still be up to you to take that deep breath and say yes to your pregnancy, and your body's inherent power.

When you do that, deeply do that, taking care of your body becomes easier, and as you take care of yourself - your spirit becomes lighter - and as your spirit becomes lighter, the whole journey of pregnancy reflects that light-filled joy!

Courage will be your fuel and will move you step by step each day of your pregnancy. You will have all you need to allow your labor to begin when you and your precious child are ready. Your labor will unfold, building in energy and intensity, and with the support of your birth team, you will step boldly into this journey.

In the worst-case scenario, some OBs view every pregnancy as a dangerous condition that can not be completed without medical intervention. There are OBs who feel that the surgical delivery of an infant is actually safer than the vaginal birth of a child through normal physiological labor - this is in spite of copious scientific evidence to the contrary.

Info on cesarean vs vaginal birth:
https://www.livescience.com/45681-vaginal-birth-vs-c-section.html

True obstetrical emergencies in healthy pregnant women/mothers are very rare. For those rare cases, access to trained surgeons is indeed a lifesaver.

The problem is that medical training treats all pregnancies as if they are the 1 or 2 percent of pregnancies that will need their aggressive support - this attitude endangers the 98%, 99% of pregnancies that will proceed smoothly through the trimesters to vigorous labor and birth of a healthy infant and a tired but overjoyed mother/parent!
How is your heart feeling now?

As you can see, there is quite a bit that's in your control. There are direct steps you can take to give yourself the best birth experience possible.

It's normal to be excited and uncertain, especially when this is your first pregnancy.

The knowledge of what's normal allows the midwife to know when things are not within normal ranges for her client. If that occurs, the midwife will refer her client to medical care. Should the need for medical assistance be seen during labor - the client will be transported to the closest hospital to complete their labor. A midwife will endeavor to make such a transfer before things are emergent and in the best interest of the health and well-being of the client. This, along with providing complete informed consent to the client, gains the birthing person/mom's consent to the transfer.

When there is a transfer, your midwives and doula will go with you to the hospital - unless COVID-19 restrictions prevent this. Please have a word with your backup hospital to be a step ahead of their restrictions.

Just to be aware and prepared. But know that most home birth and birth center babies are born at home or in the birth center of their parent's choosing - the need for transport is usually very low.

Obstetrician / Gynecologist

This is a medical doctor and trained surgeon. This person's training is in the diagnosis and treatment of the dysfunctions of pregnancy. They receive almost no training in nutrition, or in holistic wholistic means of preventing dysfunction. Overall, their training is about the worst-case scenario, and as a result, they see most pregnancies through this lens.

It speaks volumes with regard to that hospital's commitment towards a lower c-section rate and higher patient satisfaction in their births.

Be sure to ask about the rate of c-sections in any hospital you are considering for your birth - you have every right to ask and to know this information.

A certified professional midwife (CPM)

A midwife is an expert in the birthing process for healthy women/people. This person has undergone 3 or more years of training with a focus on the normal, spontaneous process of bringing a baby human, or humans, to birth.

It's important to know that the majority of women/birthing people are in this category. The midwife helps through by education about proper nutrition, exercise, and mental state that will promote health and set the stage for the healthy development of a child and its straightforward, spontaneous birth.

Midwives use low-intervention techniques to support labor - they are trained in the appropriate herbs and possibly homeopathy to be used as needed. State-licensed midwives can carry certain medications, for example, to manage bleeding after birth if the birth proves severe.

Can you imagine him/her/them guiding you through your birth process, encouraging you, supporting your partner and family, and being one of the first people to see and touch your newborn?

Midwives, what do they do?

In the United States, there are two kinds of midwives serving birthing people, Nurse Midwives (NM) and Certified Professional Midwives.

A nurse-midwife is a person who has first been is trained first as a registered nurse. After attaining this, there is further training in midwifery. This training is medically based, meaning it the training looks at pregnancy and birth as a medical event, requiring treatment. Individual training programs and individual nurse-midwives themselves may carry within them the belief that birth is a natural process for healthy pregnant women/birthing people, however, the environment of certain hospitals might prevent them from approaching birth with as much confidence as they personally might like.

Generally speaking, you can expect to spend more time talking to and connecting with a nurse-midwife. It is a very good sign when a hospital has nurse midwives on hand to attend to the needs of pregnant and birthing patients.

Doulas will also provide the hands-on support that is needed as your body proceeds through the labor process.

Your doula will support you and your, partner/husband and share with you tips and strategies to move your birth process along and encourage your relaxation and sense of safety.

In hospitals, a birth doula's constant, hands-on, care greatly reduces the need for medications and surgical delivery.

The evidence on doulas:
https://evidencebasedbirth.com/the-evidence-for-doulas/
https://pubmed.ncbi.nlm.nih.gov/18507579/

In the words of noted Dr. John Kennel, "If a doula was a drug, it would be unethical not to use it."

Some doulas are certified and some are not. Certification in and of itself is not an assurance of a knowledgeable and compassionate caregiver. Please take time to meet and talk to several doulas, ask for references, and speak to those references.

Please check in with yourself as you talk to prospective doulas and midwives. Do you feel at ease talking to this person?

My reading list will provide more information.

After doing your research, check in with yourself. How do you feel about birthing at home? In a hospital? A birthing center. Where do you imagine that YOU will feel safe?

At the end of the day - you ought to give birth where YOU will feel the most safe and have your needs as a birthing person met. This way, it will be easier for you to be present for your birth, and be courageous. Courage is certainly needed when giving birth, especially to your first child, because you have no frame of reference for the experience. and you cannot help but to be affected by the huge fear of birth that has brewed in the country. This is another reason why it's very important for your first experience to be as empowering as possible and fuel the experiences of the births of any other children you have. Or affect your desire to have another child at all!

What does a doula do?

No matter where you plan to deliver - a doula is a wonderful idea. Doulas can provide you with vital information, education, and coaching to you as you consider all of your options. Most doulas are information banks and have a good idea of the practices and reputations of the hospitals in your area and can discuss that with you. They may know the midwives in your town and can point you in the direction of the perfect provider for you!

Very often, a baby will choose to be born in the tub, and this is usually no problem if all has been going well and the mother and baby's condition are is good.

I'd like to recommend taking a look at Midwife Angelina's Facebook page as well as her Instagram account for some of the most amazing videos of spontaneous birth that I've ever seen on the internet.
https://www.facebook.com/midwifeangelina/

Hospital Birth

The majority of US children are born in a hospital. Unfortunately, the US has the worst statistics for maternal and infant mortality in the industrialized world.

Link to CDC on USA Mortality - broken down by race.
https://www.cdc.gov/reproductivehealth/maternalinfanthealth/infantmortality.htm

The US's history around birthing is steeped in racism and misogyny and the attempted destruction of midwifery in the USA is well documented and is in major part to blame for this country's mortality rates and postpartum depression rates. Racism and white supremacy have always played a huge role in causing the stress that robs Black and Indigenous women of the fire they need to birth their children in peace and power. Please educate yourself on this history.

A home birth midwife receives intensive training on the process of normal, physiological birth. They are skilled at in supporting their clients in avoiding the pitfalls of poor nutrition, stress, and lack of exercise. They are also skilled at in knowing when their clients might have a need for medical care or surgery.

This is why home birth midwives overall have excellent outcomes with their clients, and their clients report greater satisfaction with their birth experience as well as greater success breastfeeding their young ones.

Freestanding Center

A freestanding birth center is a facility run by midwives and, in no way, is it part of a medical facility. These can be nurse-midwives or certified professional midwives, or a mix of the two!

The benefit here is that a birth center can provide a homelike environment, freedom of movement, and the skill of midwifery care. There are no large machines or epidurals offered, however, the midwives keep track of the mother's and baby's progress using a doppler (handheld listening device.) or fetoscope. There is usually a large birthing tub where a mom can soak her laboring body, as well as share that space with her partner and perhaps other children.

Thoughts and Feelings:

_____

_____

_____

_____

_____

_____

_____

_____

5. Imagine your birth team

Who will support you in your pregnancy? Who will support your birth?

Feel free to research the options available here:

Homebirth

In the USA home births are generally attended by certified professional midwives (CPM) in some states licensing is also required (LM).

4. Learn about natural family planning.

Did you know that it is possible to be so acquainted with your fertility cycle that you can work with that cycle to either achieve a pregnancy or avoid one? I'll include links to books and resources that teach natural family planning in this book. Please note: that natural family planning methods have the same effectiveness rate as chemical birth control "The Pill," ,98-99 percent the 1 or 2 percent difference is due to human failure, same as The Pill, so please seek informed instruction in natural family planning methods to avoid the stress of an unplanned pregnancy. Once you have done this, once you have learned an NFP method that works for you, you know with it forever, it costs you nothing, and it has no health-threatening side effects!

I would warmly encourage such an empowering method of family planning!

An important note for Catholic Christians: NFP practiced within the context requests of our faith is completely appropriate for one choosing to live as our faith requires. This is because NFP works with our body's natural cycle as opposed to imposing a false cycle, as chemical birth control does. As long as NFP is practiced within the church's teachings on family life and sexuality, a Catholic has no need to be concerned about making use of this gift.

To receive a copy of Midwife Robin Lim's book The Natural Family Planning Workbook and support Bumi Sehat Birthing Center, please visit this website:

http://iburobin.com

Most whole protein foods come with fat naturally (no need to skin chicken or remove yokes). Good sources of fat are nuts/nut butters, seeds, avocados, olives, and raw oils like olive oil, coconut oil, and butter. Avoid fat-free and low-fat food products

How you eat right now, gives your body the building blocks needed to make your strongest decisions, and live your brightest life, with children or not.

Feel free to record your nutrition plan below:

_____

_____

_____

_____

_____

_____

_____

_____

_____

_____

_____

Good sources of whole grains are brown rice, quinoa, millet, bulgur, barley, oats, buckwheat, amaranth, kamut, spelt, rye or wheat berries, corn, and wild rice.

4. Vitamin C

Vitamin C boosts and strengthens the immune system; this helps you avoid getting sick and shortens recovery time. It does this by building and repairing soft tissue, which helps wounds heal faster. Some food sources of Vitamin C are citrus fruits, berries, grapes, cherries, kiwi, apricots, plums, bananas, apples, pears, cantaloupe, watermelon, pineapple, mango, papaya, bell peppers, tomato, carrots, cucumbers, beets, cauliflower, summer and winter squash, sweet potatoes, yams, potatoes, corn, and avocado.

5. Water

Think amniotic fluid! Water supports and replenishes the environment of your growing baby. In addition, water helps regulate body temperature, lubricates and cushions joints, protects the spinal cord and other sensitive tissue, and helps rid the body of waste through urination, perspiration, and bowel movements. Pregnant women need to drink about 10 cups of water every day. To make sure you're getting enough water, check your pee; it should be the color of light lemon juice.

Thumbs Up for Fat

Despite its bad rap, fat is essential for health. Fat removes dead cells, helps manage moods, brain function, and energy, and is essential in the digestion of veggies and other foods.

3. Learn about nutrition: The Five Finger eating plan.

"Five-finger" eating, developed by midwife Valerie El Halta, is an easy way to make sure you get the nutrition you need during pregnancy. Pregnant women need to eat all five "fingers" at each meal, 3X a day. Using this as a foundation, have fun creating and eating meals and snacks.

1. Protein

Protein is the most important part of a pregnant mama's diet. Protein builds your baby's body, placenta, umbilical cord, and amniotic sac, while at the same time maintaining every part of your body. Pregnant women need 100 grams of protein every day. Meat, fish, eggs, beans, nuts/nut butters, dairy, and certain types of soy are all sources of protein.

2. Green Leafy Vegetables

Green veggies have calcium, magnesium, iron, potassium, zinc, vitamins A, C, E, & K, fiber, folic acid, and other vitamins and minerals essential for you and your growing baby. Eating greens purifies the blood, improves circulation, strengthens respiration, helps ward off cancer, strengthens the immune system (suppressed during pregnancy), and much more. Broccoli, broccoli rabe, kale, collards, bok choy, spinach, swiss chard, watercress, cabbages, mustard greens, dandelion greens, lettuces, and arugula are all great greens.

3. Whole Grains

Whole grains are like little energy capsules. Because we absorb them slowly, they help keep us going. They are also great sources of essential enzymes, iron, fiber, vitamin E, and B-complex.

2. Prepare your body!

If giving birth is part of your life plan, I suggest living every day with this in mind.

What I mean here is that pregnancy is a possibility in any fertile and sexually active woman's life. Even if you are taking chemical birth control, that method is generally about 98% effective. That 2% means much when it results in the conception of a baby!

Knowing this, there is wisdom in taking good care of your precious body. Eat well, exercise, meditate, record your thoughts, and pray (if this is your spiritual practice), reduce stress, and savor the amazing possibilities of your body.

_____

_____

_____

_____

_____

_____

_____

_____

_____

_____

_____

1. - Feel your breath, in and out...
2. - Feel your body on the bed or chair...
3. - Slowly move your hands and feet - coming back now.
4. - and...
5. - When you are ready, open your eyes and return to
   your day. Free from fear - and full of J joy.

Please feel free to record this meditation using your own voice - I believe that there is a great deal of power in soothing and reparenting yourself into a place of wholeness and courage.

Record your thoughts after completing this exercise:

_____

_____

_____

_____

_____

_____

_____

_____

_____

_____

You are your own excellent, powerful, intelligent person. ...

You can create your own team of safety around you. ..
You can choose birth workers who celebrate your choices.
You can eat and drink well, with nutritious foods and plenty of water. ..
You can exercise, and read books about birth that inspire you. ..
You can prepare yourself for a birth that brings you peace and pleasure. ..
You can, no matter how your labor unfolds, find a place in your mind where you can enjoy, and feel the incredible power of the process. ..
You can relax, let go of fear, and allow your labor to bring your baby into your arms. ..

Ultimately, the vision of your mother's experience begins to fade - sweetly, like a mist. Slowly, the vision fades and all that is left is gratitude. Gratitude for your own life and all its your own beautiful possibilities. Gratitude for your own power - your own life - your own choices.
It is time to return to normal waking consciousness.

Focus on your breathing. In your mind, count from 1 - 5 and when you arrive at 5, you will feel refreshed, happy, and calm.

What stories was she told about birth? Was she excited? Frightened?

If your mother is deceased or if you were adopted, simply breathe deeply and allow visions and thoughts to appear to you - what might have been her state of mind, what might have been her emotional state?

Whatever appears - happy or sad - allow the visions to slowly appear. Breathe into whatever you are seeing and feeling - if you feel sadness or happiness, simply accept these emotions and be at peace within them.

Imagine Vision yourself walking in a place that brings you happiness and security - it could be a place in nature - or a place you have always wanted to go - imagine yourself there now, walking in safety and feeling every emotion or seeing whatever visions have come to you as you consider your own birth.

Imagine your mother or the essence of your mother.
Allow yourself to consider that your mother's story - is your mother's story. You are your own unique person.

You have the ability and right to have a different experience than what she had. Even if her experience was wonderful - you have the ability to have your own version of a wonderful, empowered, and safe birth experience.

BIRTH STORY MEDITATION

Pick a quiet and safe place. It could be lying on your bed or sitting comfortably in a chair. It would be best to feel completely supported, so that little to no energy is being used to hold your body up.

Feel free to have soothing music playing. If you have a favorite aromatherapy scent - please use it, either with a diffuser or incense.

Settle yourself in, and remember to turn off or down your phone so that you will not be disturbed as you begin an inward journey.

Breathe deeply;

In and out.

Let your focus be on your breath.

Feel your breathing in...and your breathing out.

Allow yourself to relax and be at peace.

Right now, there is nothing you have to do,

Or anywhere that you have to go.

Allow yourself to begin to drift and float in your own inner experience.

Allow yourself to be at peace.

As you drift and float, ...allow yourself to remember the story of your birth, shared with you by your mother. What did she tell you? How did she feel during her pregnancy?

If you are not in contact with your mother, if she is deceased, or if you were adopted, you can still explore your birth story.

You can rest in meditation with soft music playing. You might light a candle and relax. - Focus on your slow, deep breathing and imagine your birth. - What do you feel? What pictures do you see? Respond with love and care for the visions that come to you. They may come in many ways, sights, sounds, memories, feelings, and even scents...

And just as in the above scenario, imagine yourself as a little infant feeling, seeing, and sensing all that has come to you. Rejoice with the happy; comfort all that is sad.

This step is wonderful to do with the support of a therapist, doula, or hypnotherapist. A therapist is especially helpful if the visions of your birth are very troubling to you. These support people are key to reducing trauma because when you were a little one, you lived through your birth alone with no one to process your experience with. Your mother may have loved you a great deal but was too traumatized herself to comfort you. A therapist, hypnotherapist, or experienced doula can comfort you, listen to you, care for you, and witness you as you step out of a painful birth story and prepare for a joyous birth with your own baby!

STEPS TO HAVE A FEARLESS BIRTH

1. Explore your own birth.

We are imprinted with our own birth experience. If your mother is living, and you are in contact with her, ask her to tell you your birth story. This might be a wonderful moment of bonding for you and your mom. A time to really understand her and the person she was when she carried you.

If your mom is comfortable with this, tape the tale to listen to later. When you listen to or reflect upon the story, imagine yourself as the infant being born in this story. How was your mother's experience of birthing you? Was she afraid, joyful, concerned? How might those emotions have affected you? Remember, - you were a tiny new human being washed in your mom's emotions, try to imagine yourself today speaking to your infant self, you can share the joy of your birth or you can comfort your infant self as needed, you can tell yourself how happy you are that you made the journey and that you are now having a baby of your own. You can apologize to your infant self for any fear or confusion that was part of your birth story, while at the same time, you can assure the child you are carrying that you will do all you can to give birth with courage and joy!

The midwives cared for me and lent me their confidence, and this inspired me to have 2 enormously beautiful birth experiences; the births of my twin sons, David and Robert, and later, the birth of my son Joseph.

My hope is that this book can comfort and inspire you. That you are able to breathe out all unnecessary fears and anxieties and to birth your child(ren) in power and in peace.

Please feel free to reach out to me if you have any questions.
You can reach me via my website:
www.niaoaklandbetterbirthfoundation.com .
You can also visit my blog at www.doulasamsarah.wordpress.com .
I look forward to hearing from you and wish you the very best in pregnancy, motherhood, parenting, and in every area of your life.

Peace and baby blessings,

Mamisi Samsarah Morgan
Executive Director
Oakland Better Birth Foundation
Better Birth Association of Harlem
Nia Healing Center for Birth & Family Life
Shiphrah's Circle Community Doula Program
Mother of David, Robert, Joseph, and Gregory, Step-Mother to Adam, Grandmother of Jazmine, Tayvone, and Gio, Mother in love to Rachel and Chanell

Many doctors are even discouraging women away from trusting their own bodies to give birth without our being induced, even though that process guarantees a more difficult labor and the increased possibility of a surgical delivery (cesarean section).

On films and television, labor and birth are never (with the exception of the earlier seasons of " Call the Midwife") shown to be the graceful, peaceful, and powerful events that they it can be in many cases. Although I will take a moment to admire an episode of "The Handmaid's Tale," wherein a birth is depicted as an act of defiance and self-determination - a powerful scene. I hope you have had the opportunity to witness it. (Handmaid's Tale, Season 2, Episode 11, "Holly" Hulu)

When I birthed my sons 43 years ago, I did so in what was called the natural childbirth movement - so there was a strong vein of societal support within that movement for my desire for natural, unmedicated birth experiences when I birthed my sons. Even though there were a few individuals in my personal life who might have thought me crazy - there were many more who cheered me on and empowered me.

I was also very blessed to receive childbirth education from midwives - rather than educators who were in any way beholden to the medical system.

AUTHOR'S FOREWORD

Before we get started.

Hello Dear Reader,

I want to thank you so much for taking the time to read this book. My goal here is to give you a gift. I'd like to help you set aside fears you may have about pregnancy and birth. I've been a doula for over 40 years at this point, and what I've noticed in my practice over the years is that women/birthing people are more fearful of giving birth each year. This is rather sad, and there are a few reasons for this.

Overall, we birth our babies ' later in life, and we often have very little access to pregnant women and babies until we ourselves are pregnant.

Most of our friends are having very medicated births and are sharing stories that can feel very terrifying, and leave us wondering, "Why on earth would anyone want to do that?" !

Our medical professionals are more likely to regard pregnant bodies with concern and skepticism rather than with joyful anticipation.

Artist: Jazmine A. Silver,
@jazsilver.art on Instagram

Promised Mother, thank you, for bringing this baby, this gift Earth side... You got this. We BELIEVE in you.

Love, Ibu Robin ~ Grandma midwife in Bali 2020

Robin Lim CPM is a Filipina, Micronesian, American midwife and founder of Bumi Sehat, a non-profit organization in Bali, Indonesia.

Ibu (mother) Robin's books may be found here: iburobin.com

For more about Ibu Robin's work in Indonesia and the Philippines, visit: www.bumisehatbali.org

Dear Promised Mother,

 I have read and reread Samsarah's offering of love: Steps to a Fearless Birth.

 Her words are like a hug, pulling us close to her heart, and giving us much-needed comfort. We live in challenging times, and I know it's not easy to be expecting a baby right now.

 All too often, we women experience "Prenatal Scare" instead of "Prenatal Care" when we go to the doctor for a check-up. I know I did, the first time I went to the OBGYN, as a pregnant teenager, 45 years ago. I ran from that doctor and, into the care of skilled and wise midwives. It took me a lot of determination and TLC from my mother, my Filipina Lola, and my midwives, to banish the fears planted during that one prenatal scare visit with the doctor. How I wish I had had Grandmother~Doula Samsarah's book in my hands, to guide and comfort me.

 Reading Samsarah's words, I felt like I was sitting across the kitchen table from her, and she was pouring me a fragrant cup of tea and, serving me warm cookies. Every page lifted me up, and that is what support really is. This book is like a magical recipe, for helping you find your own inner knowing.

CONTENTS